A WINTER JOURNEY

by David Updike

illustrated by

Robert Andrew Parker

ANDRE DEUTSCH

Published 1985 by Prentice-Hall Inc., Englewood Cliffs, New Jersey
First published in Great Britain 1985
by André Deutsch Limited
105 Great Russell Street London WC1B 3LJ

ISBN 0 233 97850 X

For John Anoff and Goldy

Once upon a time, there was a boy named Homer. He lived in a small white house with his parents, several cats, and a dog named Sophocles. Homer and Sophocles were about the same size, the same weight, and had the same colour hair. They slept in Homer's room at night and by day they played together in the garden behind the house.

One cold winter morning, Homer's mother dropped a few silver coins into his hand and told him to go into town and get a haircut. "And take Sophocles, too," she added, "in case you get lost." And so from the safety of the back garden, Homer and Sophocles crept out through a gap in the hedge and into the world beyond. They followed the rutted path over roots and stones, past the old wooden church, the post office, the library, down a short, steep hill into town.

The sky was cold and grey, and the air was still. People were rushing in and out of shops as if something exciting were about to happen.

When Homer and Sophocles went into the barber's, the old man with white hair looked over at them.

"Is your dog getting a haircut, too?" he asked. "If not, you'd better leave him outside."

Homer reluctantly led Sophocles to the door and let him out. "Wait here," he said. "I'll be out in a minute."

Homer sat down in a big chair. The barber put a bib around his neck, pumped a shiny metal bar, and Homer rose slowly upward. With a pair of scissors and an electric razor, the barber began to snip and buzz around Homer's head.

From where he sat, Homer could watch Sophocles waiting on the pavement. He saw snowflakes floating down from the still, grey sky. At first there were only a few, but the air grew lighter and whiter, and by the time he was on the street again, everything had changed. Snow covered the ground and formed a cap of white on the top of Sophocles' head. As they trudged home, they left a trail of footsteps in the snow, but these, too, were soon buried.

The snow continued to fall that afternoon in a slow, steady veil of white. It settled silently in the bushes and on the branches of the trees, turning the bare ground of the back yard to a smooth unbroken white. Homer stood with Sophocles under the enormous elm tree, looking up at the sky from which a thousand flakes fell—floating, rising, dipping through the high, thin air. Homer bent down and picked up a handful of snow and watched it fall in a silver cloud from his cupped hands.

He got on his bicycle and tried to ride across the lawn, but the snow was too deep. He sat on the swing and swung a few times. He tried to climb the small maple tree, but the branches were too slippery. He went to the gap in the hedge and looked out: cars moved along the road with a slow, steady growl. He had never seen it snow so hard before.

Homer wanted to stay out and watch the snow fall all night, but he knew his mother would not let him. Just then, he heard her calling him.

"Homer, Homer! Dinner time!"

He sprinted across the lawn, tripped on a fallen branch, rolled over in the snow, jumped off the stone wall, and went in through the back door. Only then did he realise that Sophocles was no longer with him. He opened the door and looked out, but Sophocles was not there.

"Where is Sophocles?" he asked his mother, but she didn't know.

"Don't worry. He'll be back," she said. "He probably just went for a walk."

But Homer was not convinced. After dinner he went outside and called him.

"Sophocles, Sophocles!" he yelled, but the only answer was the sad howling of the wind. He looked for footprints in the snow, but everything had been buried. He looked out onto the street, but it was deserted. In the distance, he could hear the clatter of a snow plough and the whine of a stuck car. Homer retraced his steps across the lawn and went inside.

Later that evening, after Homer had gone to bed, his parents gave a small dinner party. As he lay in bed, he could hear the sounds of glasses clinking, his mother talking, and the wild peal of Mrs. Merson's laughter—all rising up the stairs to his room. Homer could even smell the smoke of Dr. Pulsavar's cigar. Outside, the wind continued to blow and the snow tapped against the window like a man with a long crooked stick.

Although he was tired, Homer could not sleep. Now and then he would get up and look out of the window. Snow fell through the glow of the streetlamp in the shape of a bell, dancing upward in sudden gusts of wind. The front steps of the house were white and perfectly smooth, and the porch looked like an enormous bed.

He went back to his room, lay down, and closed his eyes: he could see Sophocles sitting calmly with him in the snow, and then the yard—only a moment later—a perfect, empty smoothness. Where had he gone?

Homer pulled on a pair of heavy wool socks and crept down the back stairs to the kitchen. He found his boots standing in a little puddle and pulled them on. He put on his coat, his hat, his mittens, pulled the legs of his pyjamas over his boots, and went out into the world of a soft, impossible whiteness. Snow stung his face, and his words were swept away in the wind.

"Sophocles, Sophocles!" he called. The garden was buried, and the forsythia bush had become a giant mound of snow— like an igloo.

He struggled through the snow, past the elm tree, out through the gap in the hedge, down to where the pavement should have been. With great difficulty, he climbed over the snowbank and stood on the edge of a deserted road.

"Sophocles, Sophocles," he called again. He cupped his hands over his ears and listened. Then, in the distance, Homer heard what sounded like a dog's barking. He started off toward the town—the direction from which the barking had come. All the lights of the houses were out, the streets were empty, and the wind and snow stung his face. But there, in the wind, he heard the sound again and again. He trudged on—past the neon glow of Connally's toy shop, past the old wooden church, the library, across the railway line, and into a part of town where he had never been. The snow swirled around him and fell so fast and thick that he could hardly see. He thought he heard the barking again, but where had it come from? He stopped at a crossroads and stood in the yellow glow of a streetlamp and looked around him, but nothing seemed familiar.

A man wearing a tall fur hat and smoking a big cigar walked toward Homer, his head bowed to the wind and snow.

"Excuse me, excuse me," Homer said. "Do you know where East Street is?"

The man looked up and smiled. "Kind of late to be out in the snow, isn't it?" he said, and walked right past him, down the road.

Homer walked on. He met a woman with a scarf wrapped around her head, carrying two enormous loaves of bread.

"Excuse me, have you seen my dog?" Homer asked, but instead of replying, the woman looked down at him and laughed like a wild hyena.

Behind him, he heard the jingling of bells, as from yet another street appeared a team of horses pulling a sleigh, driven by a bearded man in a fur hat, brandishing a whip.

"Mush, mush," he shouted, snapping the whip onto the backs of the horses. Homer leaped out of the way and landed in a snowdrift. As he dug himself out, the sleigh rattled past in a cloud of snow.

Suddenly, Homer wished he were back in his bed, listening to the sounds of the party downstairs, with the wind and snow tapping on his window. He started to run, but his boots were heavy. The harder he tried, the slower he went. As he ran, he heard a familiar sound behind him. He looked back at the spinning yellow light of a giant plough, close behind him and honking its horn.

"Baroorah! Baroorah!" Its headlights shone through the swirling snow like two glowing, angry eyes. Homer tried to run faster and faster, but his boots pulled at his legs like weights. He felt as if he were running on the bottom of the sea.

"Baroorah! Baroorah!" the horn blasted. Closer and closer it came. There was nowhere for him to turn. He tried to climb a snowbank, but it was too high. He began to run again, but he tripped and hit his chin on a piece of ice. Now the machine was right behind him, as big as a house, its silver plough parting the snow in two enormous waves.

"Sophocles, Sophocles!" Homer yelled. And then he heard the sound of barking, and Sophocles leaped over the snowbank beside him.

"Climb on," Sophocles said.

Homer climbed up onto the dog's back, wrapped his arms around his neck, and Sophocles leaped up into the air. They were off—rising up over the street, the houses, the plough—flying through the wind and blinding snow. Higher and higher they rose, up through the clouds to a place where it was not snowing and a million stars sparkled down from a blue-black sky. A shining moon hung above them like a silver coin.

"Hold on tight!" Sophocles said. His hair was swept back and his ears flapped in the wind as they began to descend, plunging down through the night, sweeping through the clouds to where the town lay beneath them like a dream. The snow had stopped, and everything was white and perfectly still. Homer could see Connally's toy shop, the white spire of the church, the library, and the branches of the elm tree in his own back garden.

Then he saw his house: smoke rose from the chimney, and all the lights were out except for the one in his room. Sophocles swept down over the hedge and flew into the garden, landing gently in the snow by the back door. Homer slid off his back, opened the door, followed Sophocles in, and then went up the back stairs to his room.

"Good morning!" was the next thing he heard. He looked up as his mother walked into the room. "You slept late. Did the party keep you up?" His room was bright, and the sun shone through the frosted windowpanes from the clear blue sky.

"Good morning," Homer said, sitting up slowly, rubbing the sleepiness from his eyes. He looked out of the window into the back garden. The snow had stopped, and everything was covered in a smooth, sparkling whiteness.

"Where's Sophocles?" he asked.

"He's right here," said his mother, pointing to the floor where Sophocles lay sleeping. "One of the guests must have let him in last night. He's exhausted. He must have got caught in the storm."

Homer sat silent for a moment and then gazed out of the window once more. He remembered the moon and the stars as he flew out and up through the clouds and into the clear cold darkness on Sophocles' back.

"Oh," he finally said, smiling back into the room.

And then he jumped out of bed, got dressed, and with Sophocles close behind him, hurried down the stairs. A moment later, they both ran out through the back door of the house, out into the smooth, unbroken snow of the back garden.